C000160465

1 MONTH OF
FREE
READING

at
www.ForgottenBooks.com

By purchasing this book you are eligible for one month membership to ForgottenBooks.com, giving you unlimited access to our entire collection of over 1,000,000 titles via our web site and mobile apps.

To claim your free month visit:
www.forgottenbooks.com/free1017768

* Offer is valid for 45 days from date of purchase. Terms and conditions apply.

ISBN 978-0-331-13422-3
PIBN 11017768

This book is a reproduction of an important historical work. Forgotten Books uses
state-of-the-art technology to digitally reconstruct the work, preserving the original format
whilst repairing imperfections present in the aged copy. In rare cases, an imperfection in
the original, such as a blemish or missing page, may be replicated in our edition. We do,
however, repair the vast majority of imperfections successfully; any imperfections that
remain are intentionally left to preserve the state of such historical works.

Forgotten Books is a registered trademark of FB &c Ltd.
Copyright © 2018 FB &c Ltd.
FB &c Ltd, Dalton House, 60 Windsor Avenue, London, SW19 2RR.
Company number 08720141. Registered in England and Wales.

For support please visit www.forgottenbooks.com

THE MACDONALD COLLEGE JOURNAL

This journal is owned, edited, and published monthly by Macdonald College.

For advertising rates and correspondence concerning the advertising section write to the Advertising Representative.

BOARD OF MANAGEMENT

Chairman
W. H. BRITTAIN, PH.D.

Circulation Manager
L. H. HAMILTON, M.S.

Business Manager
T. F. WARD

Editor
A. B. WALSH, B.Sc.(Agr.)

Associate Editor
H. R. C. AVISON, B.A.

ADVERTISING REPRESENTATIVE

E. GROSS
2845 Willowdale Ave.
Montreal

Telephone ATlantic 4739

All correspondence concerning the material appearing in the MACDONALD COLLEGE JOURNAL should be addressed to
THE EDITOR,
Macdonald College, P.Q.

Subscription rates — 50c per year

EDITORIAL COMMENT

Macdonald launches a new journal! Since the old Journal of Agriculture suspended publication our English-speaking farmers have had no periodical devoted exclusively to their interests. There has been no regular medium for publishing notices of government policies, bonuses, etc., no means of rapidly disseminating information regarding fairs and other events of interest to rural people. There has been no way in which we could reach them with timely information regarding new advances in farm practice, new discoveries or timely notes on market trends or other matters of interest. Yet in these rapidly changing times all these things have become of vital importance. Hundreds of farmers have expressed to us their need of and interest in such a publication.

But the farmer is also a citizen. He and his family are interested in all matters affecting the rural community. Therefore, the new journal will have a broader appeal than the old. It will deal with three main concerns of Macdonald College — the farm, the home, and the school. In other words, this journal will deal with all those things that interest the farmer and his family.

WHY A NEW FARM PAPER?

In view of the grave and disastrous events of the past weeks the question may well be asked, "Why a new farm paper?" It is our conviction that, however the struggle may go from now on, some form of regimentation of industry is inevitable, and it may well be that the greatest amount of regimentation will be in agriculture. The need for accurate information, for guidance and for counsel, has become imperative. For the farmers of Quebec, for the people generally, a medium of publicity that will furnish them with all this is a vital necessity. The editors of this journal have taken on themselves the responsibility of keeping in close touch with the situation with the intention of passing it on to their readers. We only ask our readers to help us to help them.

WHO WILL THE JOURNAL INTEREST?

The Macdonald College Journal will serve the broad interests of the people of Quebec and adjoining areas:

For the farmer, it will furnish timely articles and notes on matters of production and of marketing and of the activities of farmers' societies and breed associations.

For the rural housewife, it will equally provide information of interest to her.

For the cooperator, it will provide educational material on the subject of cooperation and of the activities of cooperatives.

For the rural teacher, it will provide a means of keeping in touch with all matters of interest to rural schools.

For club members, it will contain valuable source material and outlines for study.

For the rural citizen, it will contain articles on all matters affecting the welfare of the rural community — social, economic and educational.

For the Macdonald College Alumni, it will contain notes of current interest regarding College activities, former students, and staff.

It has taken courage to launch this undertaking in these trying and difficult times and we shall require your support to make this venture a success. Without a large subscription list we cannot continue. If you wish to join us in this important enterprise, do not delay in sending in your subscription. The future of the Journal depends upon that!

Greetings from the Prime Minister

I welcome with pleasure the appearance of the Macdonald College Journal, and hope that the English-speaking people in the rural districts of our Province will support it. The authorities of Macdonald College, an institution whose reputation is well known throughout Canada and beyond, have organized it and are in charge of its policies. The staff of the College are all experts and are well fitted to be entrusted with the responsibility of publishing this magazine, which will contain the latest information on the subject of agriculture.

Every month, you will find several pages in the Journal which have been prepared by the Department of Agriculture, in which the policies of the officers of the Department will be announced and explained. For example, all information regarding the obtaining of grants, and participation in various competitions, will appear in these pages. This section, which in a sense will replace the old Journal of Agriculture, will be the link between the farming communities and the Department of Agriculture. All new legislation will be explained, as will the plans of each of the departmental divisions. Their recommendations will be featured. In a word, anyone who reads the Macdonald College Journal carefully cannot fail to keep up to date with what is going on in agriculture.

In view of the present campaign for increased production, it is wise, even imperative, that the farmers should keep in close contact with the institutions which exist to serve them. We must strain every effort to make our land produce as much as it can and in order to accomplish this we must have a concerted effort throughout the country. I feel certain that the Macdonald College Journal will be a splendid instrument in achieving this cooperation and I wish it a long life and a profitable career.

ADELARD GODBOUT,

Premier of Quebec.

DEPARTMENT OF AGRICULTURE

Agricultural Activities, Plans and Policies of the Quebec Department of Agriculture.

THE PLESSISVILLE LINEN-MAKING SCHOOL

THE prosperous little city of Plessisville will soon become the centre of Canadian linen production as a result of steps taken by the Hon. Adelard Godbout, Minister of Agriculture and Premier, to develop this industry among our rural people.

In a recent interview Mr. Godbout revealed that a linen school would be established at Plessisville, and also an important factory for making harvesting and processing machines for flax. A cooperative organization through which all the farmers in Quebec can process their flax crop will complete the set-up of this new governmental project.

Manufacture of the cultivating, harvesting and processing machinery is already underway at the Plessisville Foundry. Mr. Sonens, the Belgian inventor who came from the world's largest linen-producing centre at Cour-

tray, Belgium, to establish the industry in Canada, is in charge. Mr. Godbout stated that the school would be established very soon, and that it would be the only one of its kind in Canada. "It is very likely," he said, "that this will become the Canadian Linen School, since the bulk of our flax is grown in this province."

Students at the school will be able to take practical courses at the processing factory which will be established at Plessisville, and to which the farmers, organized into a cooperative society, can send their crop. The laboratories of the factory will be at their service.

The Department of Agriculture, through its agronomic service, intends to start a campaign to show the farmers how to grow flax, and Mr. Godbout believes that this industry will be a source of considerable profit to our farmers.

BILL No. 40

An Act respecting the Pledge of Agricultural Property

THIS project is to allow farmers to obtain short term loans by putting up agricultural products or domestic animals as security. Under the present law, any security offered must be seized, which makes it inapplicable to cases like the above. A registration system is provided to guard against fraud.

HIS MAJESTY, with the advice and consent of the Legislative Council and the Legislative Assembly of Quebec, enacts as follows:

1. The Civil Code is amended by the addition, following article 1979, of the following chapter and articles:

   "Chapter Three
   re agricultural hypothecation.

1979a. As security for a loan which he may contract, for a term not exceeding 18 months, any farmer may pledge any domestic animals and all products of his farm, on hand or in prospect, while still retaining possession of them. The borrower, in his relations with his creditor, acts as a trustee, without any claim against the creditor for storage or maintenance costs.

1979b. This hypothecation must be attested by a document made out in duplicate, one copy of which must be deposited in the office of the Registrar of the district in which the farm whose crops or animals have been pledged is situated.

1979c. Should the borrower fail to fulfill his obligations, the creditor, without prejudice to other means of recourse,

1. May compel the borrower to deliver to him, on demand, the articles offered as security.

2. May sell these articles at auction after at least three days notice, given at the door of the parish church at the close of the morning service (both by written notice and verbally) and sent by registered mail to the address of the debtor.

Eight days after the sale the creditor is required to make an accounting to the borrower or to his creditors of the results of the sale, and to turn over to him any surplus remaining after settlement of the debt and of any costs incurred.

1979d. Notwithstanding articles 598 and 599 of the Civil Code, the articles pledged are seizable for settlement of the amount due the creditor; it cannot be agreed that, in default of payment, the creditor shall become the owner of the articles. Once he has taken possession of them he is bound, if the borrower demands it, to turn them into cash with the least possible delay.

---

2. This law will come into force on the day of its sanction.

PASTURE IMPROVEMENT GRANTS

THE Deputy Minister of Agriculture, Mr. L. P. Roy, announces grants in aid of pasture improvement in this province. These are available to members of the Quebec Beef Cattle Association, the Dairy Herd Improvement Clubs, or participants in the Better Farming Competitions. Details of the grants and the procedure to be followed to obtain them are given below.

To members of the above associations the following grants are offered:

For an area of pasture representing ½ acre or ½ "arpent" or less per animal unit, up to a maximum of 10 acres or "arpents" according to the unit in use in the locality, the Department of Agriculture will pay for the 1st year: one-third of the cost of the seed and chemical fertilizer used; for the 2nd and 3rd year: $1.00 per acre or "arpent" of improved pasture.

Competitors must follow the recommendations of the Provincial Pasture Committee concerning the nature and the quantities of chemical fertilizer and of seed to be used on the different pasture soils. When seeding of the pasture is judged necessary, the grants will be given only for the use of Pasture Mixture No. 1. Beef cattle producers will make an annual report showing the weight or measurement of their animals at the beginning and at the end of the grazing season. Other competitors will make an annual report showing the total quantity of milk (per unit pasture area) and the number of grazing days (per unit pasture area and per animal unit) furnished by the pasture which has been entirely or partially improved.

Requests for authorization to hold contests under the present regulations must be sent to the Fertilizer and Pasture Section of the Department of Agriculture. The request should mention the number of competitors, the total nuber of pasture units to be improved during the year, and the total approximate cost of this improvement.

PUREBRED HOGS FOR QUEBEC BREEDERS

AUCTION sales of purebred hogs, such as that held at Plessisville on July 10th, offer our farmers an excellent chance to improve the quality of their animals, by obtaining high quality breeding stock at moderate cost. The importance of using parents of known quality in building up a herd cannot be overemphasized; the boars and sows used for this purpose can never possess too many good qualities.

The auction was organized by the Swine Breeders' Club of Plessisville and over 100 head were offered for sale. These were all registered animals of the best known breeds, between four and six months old, and classed as either XXX or XX. As an inducement to our farmers to purchase these animals the Department of Agriculture offered the following bonuses to buyers:

For a boar rated XXX, both of whose parents were of Advanced Registration ... $12.00

For a purebred boar rated XXX $10.00

For a purebred boar rated XX .... $ 5.00

For a sow rated XXX.......... . ... $ 5.00

THE QUEBEC PROVINCIAL FERTILIZER BOARD

THIS Board is made up of representatives from agricultural colleges, of technical agriculturists from both the Provincial and the Federal Departments of Agriculture, and members of the various fertilizer firms. Its function is to gather the latest technical information regarding soil fertilizing, to regulate the fertilizer trade for the benefit of all, and in general to act as an advisory body for the Province of Quebec in connection with its fertilizer problems. Recommendations as to the kind and amount of fertilizer to be applied for various crops and on various soils in the Province of Quebec are published from time to time.

The President of the Board is Mr. Andre Auger, Chief of the Field Husbandry Branch at Quebec; the Secretary is Mr. Roland L'Esperance, also of the Provincial Department of Agriculture, in the Fertilizer and Pasture Section. Other members are Dr. W. DeLong, Macdonald College; Charles A. Fontaine of Oka; Auguste Scott of Ste. Anne de la Pocataiere; J. A. Ste-Marie, Superintendent of the Experimental Station at Lennoxville; and Mr. B. Leslie Emslie of Canadian Industries, Limited.

THE QUEBEC SEED BOARD

The Quebec Seed Board, which originated as a voluntary organization, is now supported by the Provincial Department of Agriculture and is accepted as the official advisory board for all questions concerning seeds of field crops. The Board carries out comparative tests of many varieties to determine their characteristics, yield and general suitability for use in this province, and issues from time to time lists of recommended varieties. When a new or improved variety is developed it is tested by the Board and if it appears suitable it is added to the list of recommended varieties.

Each year the Seed Board makes an extensive study of the seed requirements and supply for the coming season, and through the farm press and the agronomic service, keeps farmers informed of the situation and makes suggestions to enable them to be sure of a supply of good seed for next year's operations.

Prof. R. Summerby of Macdonald College is Chairman of the Board, and its membership includes representatives from the agricultural colleges, experimental farms, the

Department of Agriculture, the Agronomic Service, the Dominion Seed Branch and the Canadian Seed Growers' Association. The seed producers and the seed trade are also represented.

THE PROVINCIAL PASTURE COMMITTEE

Pastures represent a very considerable asset to the stockmen of Quebec, and the Government and other interested groups carry on a great deal of experimental work to find out how our pastures may be improved and kept in the best possible condition.

The Provincial Pasture Committee represents all groups in the Province who are engaged in pasture investigations. The Chairman is Prof. L. C. Raymond of Macdonald College; Mr. R. L'Esperance of the Department of Agriculture at Quebec is the Secretary. The other members of the Committee are André Auger, L. Beaudet and S. Chagnon, of the Department of Agriculture; E. S. Hopkins of the Central Experimental Farm at Ottawa; J. E. Montreuil of the experimental station at L'Assomption; R. Pelletier, M. Proulx and A. Scott from Ste. Anne de la Pocatiere; W. S. Richardson and J. A. Ste-Marie of Lennoxville; P. E. Vezina from Oka and C. L. Wrenshall of Macdonald College.

The recommendations of the Provincial Pasture Committee for 1940 are contained in Circular No. 119, which may be obtained from the Department of Agriculture at Quebec.

THE QUEBEC AGRONOMIC SERVICE

TO Macdonald College belongs the credit for having started the system of county agricultural representatives or agnonomes. The first agents to be officially employed by the Department of Agriculture were appointed in 1913.

We give below the names of the 21 regional agronomes in Quebec. The counties over which each man has charge are shown immediately after his address.

1. J. E. Dube, Carleton-sur-Mer. Bonaventure, North Gaspé, South Gaspé, Madeleine Islands.

2. J. N. Albert, Rimouski, Matane, Matapedia, Rimouski, Riviere-du-Loup.

3. F. Champagne, Ste. Anne de la Pocatiere. Kamouraska, l'Islet, Montmagny, Temiscouta.

4. E. Brisebois, St. Romauld. Bellechasse, Dorchester, Levis, Lotbiniere.

5. J. A. Plante, St. Georges. Beauce, Frontenac.

6. J. E. Lemire, Victoriaville. Arthabaska, Megantic, Wolfe.

7. J. B. Milette, Nicolet. Drummond, Nicolet, Richelieu, Yamaska.

8. W. G. McDougall, Lennoxville. Compton, Richmond, Sherbrooke, Stanstead.

9. D. Fortin, St. Hyacinthe. Bagot, Chambly, St. Hyacinthe, Vercheres.

10. J. M. A. St. Denis, Granby. Brome, Rouville, Shefford.

11. J. A. Leclerc, St. Johns. Iberville, Missisquoi, St. John.

12. P. N. April, Ste. Martine. Beauharnois, Chateauguay, Huntingdon, Laprairie, Napierville.

13. R. P. Charbonneau, 152 Notre Dame St., Montreal. Jacques Cartier, Laval, Soulanges, Vaudreuil.

14. J. R. Gauthier, Macamic. Abitibi.

14a. L. J. Begin, Ville-Marie. Temiscamingue.

15. J. W. Delaney, Hull. Gatineau, Hull, Papineau, Pontiac.

16. J. A. Parenteau, St. Jerome. Argenteuil, Two-Mountains, Labelle, Terrebonne.

17. Ant. Charbonneau, Joliette. Berthier, Joliette, l'Assomption, Montcalm.

18. J. E. Roy, 1352 Royal St. Three Rivers. Champlain, Laviolette, Maskinonge, St. Maurice, Three Rivers.

19. Henri Lauziere, Charlesbourg. Charlevoiz, Montmorency, Portneuf, Quebec, Saguenay.

20. J. L. Langevin, Hebertville Station. Chicoutimi, Lake St. John, Roberval.

J. A. PROULX
*Chief, Extension Service,
Department of Agriculture*

PARASITES OF SHEEP IN QUEBEC

by W. E. Swales, B.V.Sc., Ph.D.

Division of Animal Pathology, Science Service, Dominion Department of Agriculture.
Institute of Parasitology, Macdonald College.

ALTHOUGH sheep flocks in the province of Quebec are exposed to more dangerous parasites than are flocks in other parts of Canada, at least some of the reasons for fearing these important causes of loss appear to have been removed.

A programme of research work was commenced in the Institute of Parasitology in 1936 and was later fostered by Le Comité des Recherches Agricoles, Quebec Department of Agriculture, and by the Dominion Department of Agriculture. This work has led to certain developments that give promise of complete control of the most important parasitic diseases of sheep in eastern Canada. Experiments conducted with the cooperation of many individuals, and work involving the detailed post-mortem examinations of nearly one thousand sheep- and the study of over three million individual parasites, have resulted in a clearer view of the problems and their solutions. The results can now be stated briefly, as follows:—

DANGEROUS PARASITES AND THE DISEASES THEY CAUSE

(1) Twenty-one species of worm parasites appear commonly in sheep and lambs in the Province of Quebec; of these, at least four are capable of causing actual disease and consequent losses.

(2) The four dangerous parasites are the "Twisted-wire" stomach worm, the hookworm, the microscopic intestinal worm and the nodular worm. The effects of these parasites constitute three well defined diseases, Wireworm Disease, Black Scours and Nodular Disease.

(3) *Wireworm Disease* occurs chiefly in lambs in July, August and less frequently in September. It is characterized by a sudden appearance, by anaemia (as detected by pale eye membranes) and by constipation. Animals may die quickly if they are badly infected. Fortunately little if any infection survives on pasture over the winter months and the parasites in the stomachs of infected animals are easily destroyed. A drench of a 2% solution of copper sulphate containing 1½% of nicotine sulphate, given in two ounce doses to adult sheep and in half to one ounce doses to lambs, is highly effective. All adult sheep should be treated each spring before they contaminate the pastures, and lambs should be treated in early July and again in August. A full description of methods is given in the Dominion Department of Agriculture Publication 639 (Farmers' Bulletin 69).

(4) *Black Scours* appears in lambs and young stock in October or November and will continue into the winter. This disease is characterized by a dark, foul smelling diarrhoea; the affected animal gradually loses weight, has dirty hind quarters and dry, rough wool. Affected animals do not usually die but they remain unthrifty and are usually sold as "culls" during the winter. The infection on the pasture is able to survive over the winter months, hence complete elimination of the responsible parasites is not possible. Regular dosing with the copper-nicotine drench, with capsules of tetrachlorethylene or other remedies of good reputation, reduces the infection to a considerable extent. However, this disease apparently does not occur when animals have good pasture with no mineral deficiencies, and where stocking of land is not too heavy.

(5) *Nodular disease* can ruin a flock by making ewes of only three or four years of age unable to thrive on winter feed. In some areas in this province it will also affect lambs to such an extent that they cease to thrive after the beginning of September and soon become "culls". In badly infected flocks the intestines become literally covered with hard, pea-sized nodules and sometimes the valve connecting the small intestine with the large intestine is almost blocked. Affected ewes will often thrive on grass but will become very unthrifty on dry winter feed; in such cases the diet of hay cannot be economically utilized by the injured intestine and the animal scouts and if it does not abort will be unable to raise healthy lambs.

A NEW TREATMENT FOR NODULAR DISEASE

Until very recently there was no means of preventing nodular disease other than by pasture rotation and careful management. Our recent work has indicated that complete control is possible because the winter destroys the pasture infection and the development of a practical means of using a highly effective new drug, *phenothiazine*, enables us to remove the worms from breeding stock in the early spring. Although the final tests will not be completed until the autumn of this year it seems highly probable that this new means of treatment will protect our flocks against this wasteful parasite. It is hoped that tablets of phenothiazine will soon be made available at a relatively low cost.

Although treatments to prevent parasitic disease of sheep are very necessary, it must be remembered that they are not intended to replace good husbandry. Even parasite-free lambs cannot thrive on deficient or overstocked pastures. Remember that a parasite causes disease only by accident — and that such accidents are usually brought about by our inattention to rules of good husbandry.

SILAGES – OLD AND NEW
by L. C. Raymond

When silage is mentioned, we generally think of corn, but the larger grasses, and legumes such as red clover and alfalfa, may also be used. Methods for making the best use of these materials are discussed in this article.

WE have become accustomed, through extensive usage over a period of years, to associate silage making almost exclusively with the corn crop. While this has been to a large extent true, quite a number of other crops have been and still are being used, in a limited way, to supply this valuable winter feed for livestock. The most recent additions to possible silage crops include those which have ordinarily been used for hay, such as the larger growing grasses and the legumes, like red clover and alfalfa.

Before discussing this subject in any detail it will be well to consider what the essential features of good silage really are. Forgetting for the moment the many minor details, there are two main requirements, which are tight packing in an air-tight container and a plentiful supply of fermentable carbohydrates. The former is satisfactorily taken care of by the familiar tower-type silo in such common use. The very height of the structure insures close packing, due to the weight of the green material, but this is usually supplemented by tramping during the filling process. Cutting the green herbage into short lengths facilitates both the loading and unloading of the silo as well as the packing, but is not essential to producing good silage. The second requirement having to do with the supply of fermentable carbohydrates may or may not be met by the material ensiled. Carbohydrates are mainly the starches and/or sugars which have been built up in the plant tissue. Just as soon as the herbage is placed in the silo the bacteria always present on green plant tissues become active. The tight packing excludes oxygen and the so-called anaerobic bacteria function. There is an immediate temperature rise and carbon dioxide is formed, which reaction leaves as an end product mainly acids, mostly lactic acid and a small amount of acetic acid. This rise in acidity goes on till a pH of between 3 and 4 is reached, which is sufficiently acid to preserve the fodder in its air-tight container.

STORING OF GRASS SILAGE

Success in silage-making is determined largely by the character of the herbage ensiled; either the carbohydrates must be supplied in the material itself or from some other source if the normal process is to proceed. Corn is practically ideal from this standpoint; grasses have less carbohydrate and more protein, while legumes are the most difficult of the lot to ensile, due to lack of proper balance between protein and carbohydrate.

Recognizing the difficulties attending the making of hay from grasses, and particularly the legumes, ways have

GENERAL VIEW OF THE SET-UP FOR GRASS SILAGE AT THE LENNOXVILLE EXPERIMENTAL STATION.

been sought of storing this crop in some way other than that usually employed. Extensive trials, mainly in Europe, have been devoted to immediate, artificial drying, and while a very good product has resulted, the cost has so far prevented general use of this method. Ordinary hay-making methods were very destructive of the high vitamin content of the natural herbage. The quick drying process overcame this but when the dried product was stored for only a short time it also became depleted.

THE A.I.V. PROCESS

In an attempt to overcome these difficulties resort was had to some method of ensiling grass and legume crops. Prof. A. I. Vitanen is usually credited with devising the first practical means to make them into good silage. He argued, and quite rightly, that if it was the acids formed by the action of bacteria which preserved the natural silage, then it would be simpler and more efficient to add acid at once, since bacteria introduce a destructive action resulting in loss of food nutrients. He therefore proposed the use of suitable quantities of the two strong acids, sulphuric and hydrochloric. The quantities added varied with the nature of the material. Various difficulties are involved in this process. It is not at all easy to determine the exact amount of acid required for any given lot of herbage and the strong acids are very destructive, requiring special handling in suitable containers. Repeated investigations have, however, shown that this so-called A.I.V. process is the most efficient yet devised for the preservation of green herbage. In spite of this, the troubles attending the ensiling operation have not made it a popular practice on this continent.

DETAIL OF THE FEED-BOX AND MOLASSES SUPPLY.

A modification of the A.I.V. method has been in use for several years which employs phosphoric acid instead of the more caustic sulphuric and hydrochloric. Phosphotic acid is sufficiently mild in its action to permit its passage through the metal cutter, thus avoiding one of the main handicaps of the A.I.V. process. The principle involved is exactly the same but there are some important advantages. Phosphorus is an important food nutrient, generally lacking in our forage. It therefore increases feeding value, preserves the forage, and any not so employed is excreted by the animal and is returned as a fertilizer.

THE MOLASSES METHOD

By far the most popular system of preserving grasses and legumes as silage is the addition to the cut herbage of ordinary feed molasses. This involves an entirely different principle to the use of acids. Acids prevent bacterial activity almost entirely, while molasses stimulates their activity, since it means the addition of a readily fermentable carbohydrate, largely in the form of sugar. The molasses method, therefore, simply makes up the carbohydrate deficiency in the herbage and allows the normal process to proceed. Molasses can be applied through the cutting-box; in fact, the modern cutters are fitted with an ingenious connection to regulate the rate of flow in proportion to the amount of fodder going through. Since it is quite viscous it is invariably diluted, usually with warm water, to provide better flow. The quantity required varies with the particular kind of herbage and also with its condition, mainly its maturity. Depending on these factors, the amount used may be anywhere from 40 to 100 lbs. per ton. Grasses require less than legumes and early cut herbage more than that which is more mature. Red clover, for example, in the early bloom stage, requires from 60 to 80 lbs. per ton. In this method, as with phosphoric acid, a food product is being added and while there is considerable

breakdown, the food value of the added molasses is not by any means lost.

The added cost of making grass and legume silage, due to the addition of one or other aid to preservation, is a matter for consideration. At the present time molasses provides the cheapest means. In drums molasses costs anywhere from 1¼ to 1½ cents per lb., which would mean a cost per ton of a dollar to a dollar and twenty cents where 80 lbs. is required. The A.I.V. introduces a slightly higher cost, while phosphoric acid will in most instances cost the most of the three methods.

TIME OF CUTTING IMPORTANT

The maturity of the crop to be ensiled introduces a number of factors of importance. With both grasses and legumes, the earlier they are cut the higher is the feeding value since their protein content diminishes rapidly with age. The yield of the crop must nevertheless be considered and very early cutting reduces sharply the quantity obtained from a given area. In practice this has resulted in allowing the crop to reach the early heading stage so as to provide a proper balance between yield and maturity. When harvesting at a relatively early stage some difficulty is often experienced through seepage, due to the high moisture content. This seepage carries with it much valuable nutrient and should be prevented if possible. Partial wilting of the herbage before ensiling will help to prevent this trouble. Care must be taken, however, to avoid overdoing the wilting, since this causes a loss in vitamin supply.

We may now appropriately ask where this newer silage fits into the scheme of farm management in eastern Canada? The answer is to the legumes and particularly to the red clover crop, which is the most universally grown. Where made into hay, red clover is commonly allowed to become too mature, a condition which is frequently associated with lodging and much loss of leaf and which finally results in a hay much below the potential value of the original crop. Cut for silage at the early bloom stage, there is usually no lodging or leaf loss. Several things are accomplished by cutting red clover at this time. It spreads the work of harvesting, since the desired stage is reached around the 15th to 20th of June; it allows the most complete preservation of the crop; it furnishes a high quality feed which may be used to supplement the summer pasture, or held over for the winter, and it provides an abundant aftermath which may be used for hay, for more silage, or carried over as a seed crop.

The corn crop, in districts where it is adapted, should probably still furnish the bulk of the winter roughage feed, but there is a real opportunity now available to consume more completely crops we can and do grow readily and at the same time vastly improve the winter ration for our stock.

SWINE FEEDING
by E. W. Crampton
PART I.—SWINE FEEDS

THE general problem of swine feeding may with advantage be considered under three main headings, namely, Swine Feeds, the Nutritional Requirements of Swine and Feeding Practice. Each of these sections is more or less a subject in itself, which may be discussed as a unit. In the first two articles, we shall deal primarily with the nature and peculiarities of the several feeding stuffs which may be used in the computing of suitable hog rations.

FEEDING TERMS — NUTRIENTS

Before starting on a discussion of feed stuffs, however, there are a few terms especially useful in describing feeds and feeding practice which it will be advisable to define, since every feeder should be familiar with them. A NUTRIENT is any part of a feed stuff which provides nourishment to an animal. Thus PROTEIN, that part of a feed necessary for producing lean muscle, skin, wool, etc., is a nutrient. FATS, the oily part of feeds, and CARBOHYDRATES, represented by starches and sugars, are nutrients used chiefly for body fuel and for energy for work. None of the nutrients are completely absorbed from the intestines into the blood stream. Hene we find that eaten protein for example may be 75% absorbed or DIGESTED. When the quantities of the primary nutrients, protein, fat and carbohydrate, which are digested, are added together their total is referred to as the TOTAL DIGESTIBLE NUTRIENTS of that feed or ration.

It must be remembered that the term nutrient applies also to the mineral elements needed by the animal, such as calcium, phosphorus, salt, iron or iodine; and also to the vitamins.

CLASSIFICATION OF FEEDS — BASAL FEEDS

In view of their special feeding properties, swine feeds fall naturally into four groups. The first of these is sometimes referred to as the "basal feed" group, and includes those feeds which are used in large quantities in pig rations and, therefore, in a sense, form the basis of the diet. Farm grains are typical representatives of the basal feeds. Technically, these feeds are known as basal feeds because they are used chiefly to supply the carbohydrate part of the diet. Carbohydrates, such as starches and sugars, are the chief source of energy and body fat in the ration.

HIGH PROTEIN FEEDS — PROTEIN SUPPLEMENTS

A second group of swine feeds are classed as "protein supplements". Feeds of this group differ from the basal feeds, in that they are composed chiefly of protein rather than carbohydrate. Protein feeds are used in much smaller proportions in the ration than are basal feeds. In general,

only one pound of a protein supplement would be used with eight or nine pounds of the basal feed. High protein feeds are much more expensive than basal feeds and hence there is seldom a tendency to use them to excess. Rather the difficulty is more likely to be that they are used in too meagre amounts. Balancing a ration is primarily a matter of putting together high protein feeds and basal feeds in the correct proportions to supply the animal's needs.

High protein feeds have another peculiarity in feeding. They may be burned in the body to supply energy and body fat, but carbohydrates and fats cannot be used in place of protein for the production of muscle tissues or lean meat in the pig carcass. It should be mentioned in this connection, however, that there is a minimum proportion of protein in the diet below which satisfactory growth or even health in the animal cannot be maintained. The supplying of the proper quantity of protein itself is just as important as the supplying of enough total feed. Indeed, the amounts of foods of various kinds which are needed by the animal are no indication whatsoever as to how important that particular food may be in the complete nutrition of the animal.

MINERALS

The third group of feeds are used to supply certain necessary mineral elements and are called "mineral supplements". All of the natural feed stuffs contain needed minerals, but unless the entire plant is included in the ration the amounts of minerals of the diet may fall short of the animal's requirements. Thus, while the oat plant, especially if fed when immature, may be a reasonably complete diet for animals equipped to live on such foods, the seed of the oat plant is by no means complete in its assortment of nutrients required by animals. Grains and their by-products in general are deficient in calcium and phosphorus. These two minerals in particular are required for the normal growth of the skeleton. With pig rations consisting as they do largely of cereal grains, some special provision must be made for correcting this deficiency of calcium and phosphorus. Common salt must also be supplied and under certain conditions also iron and iodine.

The proportions in which mineral supplements appear in the diet are even smaller than is the case with protein supplements. Furthermore, there are sources of the most usually required minerals which are quite inexpensive. The preparation of a ration properly fortified with minerals is therefore neither difficult nor expensive and there is little excuse for the use of rations deficient in this respect.

Continued on page 21

HOW TO CURE TROUBLE IN THE BINDER

by L. G. Heimpel

THE grain binder belongs to that kind of harvesting machinery on our farms which usually stands idle for a period of ten months and then must work at high pressure for about two months of the year. While binder users usually get along remarkably well with these machines, they not infrequently are subjected to baffling troubles which often cause serious loss of time and money due to the failure to get crops cut in time.

While we frequently think of the grain binder as one machine of many parts, it is easier to locate and correct trouble, when it occurs, if we divide the machine up into its component systems, which may be outlined as follows: First there is the power delivery system which consists of the bull wheel from which power is transmitted to the countershaft by means of the main drive chain which runs on the bull wheel sprocket and the small sprocket on the countershaft. So long as the sprockets of the power delivery system are kept in good alignment and the drive chain is kept running in the right direction and at the proper tension, trouble is not likely to be serious in this system.

The cutting system of the binder comes next and the principles which apply to the operation of a mower cutter-bar also apply to that of a binder. It should be noted that the stroke of a binder knife is twice as long as that of a mower. At one end of the stroke of the knife the cutting section should stand exactly centred in a guard, then in passing to the other end of the stroke the knife passes through one guard and stops in the centre of the next one. Excessive wear in the piston bearings will shorten the stroke of the knife and will cause pounding which is very hard on the knife; it is likely to break the head off the knife if it is allowed to persist and if the guide plates permit too much up-and-down play for the knife head. Binder knives should be kept sharp, and the guards must be kept well aligned so that the knife will ride snugly on all the ledger plates of the guard. The clips holding the knife down in proper position are usually in first class adjustment in the new binder but in old binders it is occasionally necessary to bend them down so that the knife will be held down to its proper place on the ledger plate. A binder in which the cutter-bar and knife are not in good condition will pull very hard, causing excessive strain on the main drive system and an unnecessary load on the horses.

The next system in a binder might be called the "conveyor" or the "canvasses" which carry the cut grain to the binding part. Modern binders are so built that very little trouble with the platform canvas is now experienced. The elevators also give very little trouble, yet it sometimes happens that the platform canvas keeps crowding to one side of the platform exposing the opposite ends of the

roller; this is often due to unequal stretching of the canvas itself, and before any changes are made in the adjustment of the rollers the ends of the canvas should be tested for squareness. If they are out of square they should be trimmed. If the elevator canvasses start to crowd to one side it is usually because the rolls are not parallel to each other, or are out of square. On all binders the elevator frame can be adjusted to keep it square. Measuring diagonally across the elevator frame from the under side of the upper roller to the upper side of the lower roller is the best way to test this out. The two diagonals must be of the same length, and if they are not, they must be adjusted by means of the rod provided for this purpose. Make certain that the lock nuts are drawn up snugly after this adjustment. Allowing canvasses to run at all when they show a tendency to crowd to one side soon causes the ends of the slats to catch, tearing the edge of the canvas and quickly ruining it.

THE BINDING SYSTEM

The best way to ascertain what causes binding part trouble is to become thoroughly familiar with the operation of the machine when it is in good working condition. Possibly the best way to learn this is to study carefully the various operations when the binder ties a knot. To do this proceed as follows:

1. Before any grain comes into the space occupied by the bundle the binder must be properly threaded; the end of the twine must be in its place in the eye of the needle and the end must be properly gripped in the twine holder or twine disc in the knotter. The grain may now be delivered to the packers and, when sufficient has been

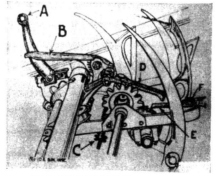

FIG. 1. MASSEY-HARRIS BINDING PART DRIVE.
A—COMPRESSOR FINGER; B—TRIP LEVER; C—TRIP LEVER SPRING ADJUSTMENT; D—DRIVING DOG STOP ARM; E—DRIVING DOG CHECK SPRING. F—DRIVING DOG CHECK ADJUSTMENT.

gathered in the bundle to overcome the tension of the trip spring, the binding parts are set in motion. In making this study it is best to turn the discharge arms by hand, slowly, so as to operate the knotter.

2. The needle will be seen to make a quick passage over the bundle and to place the other twine in a notch in the twine disc; if a loop of twine is drawn from the needle and held in the left hand the twine disc will be seen to make a partial turn, holding the two ends of the band fast. This is one of the important points in the tying of the knot. The tension of the cord holder or twine disc spring must be tight enough to keep the twine from pulling out and yet loose enough to let the bill hook pull the twine out of its grip a little when it is tying the knot.

3. The bill hook now turns, carrying the two cords around with it; when its revolution is almost complete the bills close on the cords holding them tightly. At the same time the knife will be seen to come forward to cut the twine. In some binders the knot is then forced off the bill hooks by a stripper, while in others the bills are inclined at such an angle that a stripper is not necessary, the band being pulled off the bills by the weight of the bundle under the kick of the discharge arms. The Deering binder has a stripper while the Massey-Harris has none.

4. The needle now goes back to its place below the deck. The discharge arms go back to their position of rest and the binding part is ready for another bundle.

The operator should study these events and should try to trace the motion of each part to its cause. For instance, he will find that the twine holder is held down against the twine disc by a fairly heavy spring with an adjustment nut. If this spring is under too much tension it will not allow the twine to pull through when the bill hook tries to pull out enough twine to tie the knot. If the spring is too loose, the band is pulled out before the knot is tied. It will also be seen that there is a definite relationship between the action of the bill hook and that of the other parts of the machine, everything being timed so that things are done in proper sequence, all of which suggests gear-driven parts. Gears and chains, are, by the way, the only kinds of drives by which correct timing can be accomplished and maintained.

The knotter is a very ingeniously worked out piece of mechanism. When the tyer wheel turns part of a revolution the gear on its side comes in contact with the little pinion attached to the bill hook. Then, when the bills are beginning to turn, the moveable bill will be seen to open for the rear end of the moveable bill carries a guide roller which is forced to travel along a specially prepared path. This governs its opening and closing action. The amount of tension the bills are given depends upon the adjustment of the bill hook spring. Too much tension on this spring means that the knot will stay on the hook and the band will be broken. Too little tension means that the ends of the twine will be cut but the knot will not be completed and the band will be pulled from the bills in that condition.

The best way to detect the cause of tying troubles in a binder is to examine the bands of the bundles which have been missed. The accompanying drawing (Fig. 3) shows the story the bands tell.

Band No. 1 has a knot in one end and both ends are cut off square. If found on the bills it signifies too little tension on the twine disc and probably too much tension on the twine at the twine can. To cure the trouble tighten the tension screw on the twine disc, a quarter of a turn at a time, and loosen the tension on the twine at the can.

If this band is found with the bundle, the cause is not too loose a twine disc but too much tension at the twine

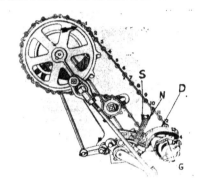

FIG. 2. FROST & WOOD BINDING PART DRIVE.
G—DRIVING DOG; D—DRIVING DOG STOP ARM; N—TRIP LEVER ADJUSTMENT; S—TRIP LEVER SPRING.

can. Sometimes this trouble is not noticed until the stooker tries to pick up a bundle, when it pulls open, showing that the bill had pulled one cord entirely from the twine disc and tied a slip-knot around it with the other cord. To cure the trouble, tighen the disc spring, a quarter of a turn at a time. If these adjustments do not stop the trouble it is possible that wear on the bill hook shaft has allowed the bill hook to drop or that the roller controlling the action of the upper bill has become worn so that the bills do not open far enough to grasp both cords at once and one may be missed occasionally. If the bundle missed occurs with regularity such as the missing of every fourth, fifth or sixth bundle, it is likely caused by wear in certain notches of the twine disc.

Band No. 2. Note that one end of the band is cut off squarely, the other being torn off. This band is found on the bills and is due to the twine tension on the can being too tight; the tension on the twine disc spring is also too great, causing the disc to crush the twine. When the needle comes up to place the twine around the bundle the twine is torn from the disc before it can be pulled from the can. The bill hook then has only one cord to tie with, so that a single knot is the result. The remedy is to relieve these tensions.   *Continued on page 21*

THE WOMEN'S INSTITUTES PAGE

A section devoted to the activities of the Quebec Institutes and to matters of interest to them.

THE 1940 CONVENTION

THE 27th consecutive annual convention of the Quebec Women's Institutes was held at Macdonald College on June 26th and 27th with an attendance of over one hundred delegates.

Mrs. Cameron E. Dow, Provincial President, presided over the opening session on Tuesday evening, which was held in the college Assembly Hall. An address of welcome to the members of the convention was given by Dr. W. H. Brittain, Vice-Principal of the College, who stressed the importance of the work of the Women's Institutes, and pointed out that in the midst of present world-shattering events every effort must be made to strengthen and intensify the programmes of the Institutes and adapt them to present needs. As proof of the continued interest of the Collège in rural life in Quebec Dr. Brittain announced that the McGill Travelling Libraries had been transferred to Macdonald College, and that a new magazine, the Macdonald College Journal, was being launched to serve the interests of the farm, the home, and the school.

Mrs. Charles Smallman, Provincial Vice-President, replied to the address of welcome. Mrs. G. S. Walsh,' Provincial Convenor of Home Economics, presented her report, which was followed by a talk by Mr. O. A. Beriau of the Department of Handicrafts in the Provincial Government, on "The Fireside Industries of Quebec."

The Honourary President, Mrs. C. E. Petch, presided over the Wednesday morning session, which was featured by an address on Nutrition by Miss Margaret McCready, the new Director of the School of Household Science at Macdonald College and by the introduction to the convention of Miss Edna Rettie, the recently appointed demonstrator for the Women's Institutes. The "Neighbour Night" programme on Wednesday evening was a great success and served to emphasize the close cooperation between the work of the Adult Education Service and the educational work of the Women's Institutes. The subject considered was "Education in Quebec" and included in the discussion were Miss Beryl Truax, President of the P.A.P.T.; Miss Adele Languedoc of the Travelling Libraries; Mr. W. A. Steeves, Headmaster of Macdonald High School; Miss Alice Dresser, Convenor of Education and Better Schools; Mrs. R. Thompson, Convenor of Adult Education. Mr. R. Alex. Sim, of the Adult Education Service, acted as chairman.

The convention was informed that the task of registering the womanpower of Canada had been assigned to the Women's Institutes, and that the dates set for this purpose were July 8th to 13th. Mrs. G. W. Kuhring, Provincial

MRS. CAMERON E. DOW

Convenor of Canadianization and Colonization distributed registration blanks to all county presidents.

The following departmental reports were presented: Agriculture, by Mrs. R. W. Hodgins; Legislation, by Mrs. A. E. Abercrombie; Canadian Industries, by Mrs. D. J. MacIntosh; Immigration and Colonization, by Mrs. Ira Merrifield; Child Welfare and Public Health, by Mrs. Lucy Daly; Publicity, by Mrs. Elizabeth McCurdy. Miss Abbie Pritchard, Provincial Treasurer, presented an audited report of the finances of the Provincial Institutes, supplemented by the findings of the Finance Committee. A more satisfactory and stable financial basis for the coming year was indicated.

Few executive changes were made. The department of Education and Better Schools was combined with Adult Education with Mrs. R. Thompson in charge. Mrs. Charles Smallman was named First Vice-President, and Miss Alice Dresser Second Vice-President. All other convenors remain in office for another year.

Group discussions on the work of the departments of the Women's Institutes, led by the officers and convenors, and stirring addresses by Mrs. Ruth B. Shaw, Canadian Supervisor of Junior Red Cross, and by Miss Hyndman, which stressed Canada's war needs, closed a very successful convention.

DESIGNS FOR LEARNING

*What dream shall I dream and what labour shall I undertake? I answer, "The first thing to do
is to create and realize the feeling for the community and to break up the petty isolation of
man from man" — AE.*

ADULT Education provides a basis for people of different racial, political and religious affiliations to work together for the enrichment of their common life. Adult Education represents a belief that people can and will work together to help themselves.

Adult Education is concerned with all parts of life. It includes helping people to meet adverse economic conditions. It means breaking down social barriers that make against a unified community. It encourages the appreciation of music, arts and crafts. Adult Education is the way

in which people equip themselves to enjoy the struggle of life, by continuing their education, by making up for what they have missed in education, by developing skills and crafts, by widening their appreciation and understanding of the world they live in.

The Rural Adult Education Service is an activity of the committee on Adult Education of McGill University; the actual direction comes from Macdonald College. The present centre of activity is at Lennoxville where Alex Sim is in charge.

NEW DEMONSTRATOR APPOINTED

MISS EDNA B. RETTIE, B.H.S., who has been appointed to the position of Demonstrator with the Quebec Women's Institutes, was warmly welcomed when introduced at the annual convention.

Miss Rettie is a graduate of Macdonald College, and during her college years was a most energetic and dependable worker. She was entrusted with considerable responsibility by her fellow students; was Vice-President of the Students' Council in her final year, and was instrumental in forming a Macdonald Branch of the McGill Red Cross Society.

THE ADULT EDUCATION COUNCIL

At an organization meeting on June 12th the Eastern Townships Adult Education Council was formed. It is an affiliation of the various groups interested in that extended section of the province and will make possible a cooperation in planning and effort not heretofore known.

Among those taking part in the meeting were; Dr. W. H. Brittain of Macdonald College who outlined ways in which the Council might function; E. C. Amaron, Principal of Stanstead College who urged the necessity "not only of thinking of the present crisis, but also of thinking and planning for the period of reconstruction which will follow the war". Representatives of Women's Institutes, Farmer's Clubs, teachers' associations, libraries, study groups, listening groups, the Federal and Provincial Departments of Agriculture, the McGill Alumni Association and Macdonald College were present.

E. C. Amaron was elected interim-President of the Council and Alex. Sim, as secretary. County committees were set up in Compton, Richmond, Sherbrooke and Stanstead.

The first work of these committees will be the planning and organizing of adult schools which will meet one night a week for six or eight weeks in the early fall. Following these schools the local study groups will be set up which will meet during the winter.

Miss Nora Bateson, who has successfully organized regional libraries in British Columbia, Prince Edward Island and Nova Scotia, told the members of the new Council of her work and showed them the possibilities of this service. The further development of libraries will be one of the matters that will engage the attention of the council at an early date.

TRAVELLING LIBRARIES
WHAT THEY ARE — HOW THEY MAY BE OBTAINED
by Adele deG. Languedoc

THE need for adequate library service in the Province of Quebec is becoming more and more acute. It is hoped that the steps recently taken in this direction in the Eastern Townships will lead to a widespread development of the regional library system. Meanwhile the Travelling Library Department of McGill University, now situated at Macdonald College, is doing pioneer work for those sections of the province cut off from library facilities, or having inadequate book collections.

In 1901, Mr. Gould, at that time Librarian of McGill University, succeeded in interesting the late Mr. Hugh McLennan in a project for establishing a travelling library system. The Hugh McLennan Travelling Libraries gave McGill the distinction of being the first, and for many years the only University in Canada to provide a service of this kind.

During the first year, and for a considerable time subsequently these little red boxes of books were sent out to rural communities from the Atlantic to the Pacific coasts. Gradually the other provinces saw the necessity of providing a library service of their own, and McGill limited its territory accordingly. The work is now concentrated in the Province of Quebec, New Brunswick, and some parts of Nova Scotia.

The scope of the work is wide, the aim being to serve people of all ages. The book collection is divided into two general classes, juvenile and adult. In the juvenile section are books suitable for school libraries; picture books for the tiny tots, nursery rhymes, games, song books, kindergarten projects, plays, etc., as well as reference books and supplementary and recreational reading of a more advanced type.

Many rural teachers have obtained Travelling Libraries from McGill University in the past and in the new quarters at Macdonald College it is expected that the service may be brought to the attention of a greater number of graduates of the School for Teachers. If a knowledge of, and a desire for, good reading can be planted in the hearts and minds of the coming generation, the work of adult education will be greatly facilitated. We have seen only too clearly in recent months how firmly the worst propaganda can take root in the infant and adolescent mind. Let us therefore make use of this method with a constructive result in view.

The adult section covers a wide field of general reading, fiction and non-fiction, and its resources have been called upon by Women's Institutes, study groups, Workers Educational Associations, Young Peoples' Societies, industrial plants, as well as by groups of individuals in isolated communities. This year there has been an increase of fifty per cent over last year in the number of boxes sent to public libraries, who find the use of Travelling Libraries

an excellent means of supplementing their book stock. To obtain one of these libraries containing 40 books the cost is nominal. For a fee of Four dollars ($4.00) the Library may be retained for a period of four months.

The fee for school libraries is two dollars ($2.00) only, as the Quebec Department of Education gives a yearly grant to cover half the fee on all libraries sent to rural schools under its jurisdiction. Transportation charges for school libraries are paid both ways by the Travelling Library Department, and the books must be housed in the school itself.

The books are not kept in fixed collections, each box being made up individually from selections submitted by the subscriber. The only restriction is that no library may contain more than one-half fiction. Any group may apply for more than one library at a time; in some instances as many as five sets have been loaned to one subscriber. In areas such as the north shore of the St. Lawrence, Lake St. John, and the mining districts of Northern Quebec, where Travelling Libraries provide the only reading matter available, the possibility of obtaining a large number of books and of changing the stock three times a year, is extremely advantageous.

Classified catalogues of the juvenile and adult collections, application forms and copies of the rules governing the loan of the Libraries are available upon request to the Travelling Library Department, Macdonald College, P.Q.

BOOK NOTES

CO-OPERATION — All those who listened to the Co-operation broadcasts on the C.B.C. last winter will be pleased to know that the script of this interesting series is available in book form at a cost of 50 cents a copy. In addition to the actual text of the broadcasts, biographical notes of the speakers, notes and references which will be of great value to the student of Co-operation, are all included. This book is available from

The Rural Adult Education Service,
Lennoxville, Quebec.

PAMPHLETS — other pamphlets recently received are available and ready for distribution. The following are some of the titles:

HOW WE GOVERN OURSELVES, Contemporary Affairs pamphlet, by G. V. Ferguson, The Ryerson Press, Toronto. (25 cents).

THE FRENCH CANADIAN PRESS AND THE WAR, Contemporary Affairs Pamphlet, by Florent LeFebvre, The Ryerson Press, Toronto. (25 cents).

WAR FINANCE IN CANADA, Contemporary Affairs Pamphlet, by F. H. Brown, J. D. Gibson and A. F. W. Plumptre, The Ryerson Press, Toronto. (75 cents).

EDUCATION FOR DEMOCRACY
Dean W. H. Brittain
Vice-Principal, Macdonald College

TO many people education means something that is "done to us" in school. Whether a person finishes his formal schooling at the seventh grade or only at the end of a university career, the result is too often the same. He puts away his books and with them the habit of learning, and settles down to what he considers the real business of life. But it is conceded that the success of democratic government depends upon the existence of an informed, intelligent, and honest electorate, and in times like these it is well to ask ourselves how nearly we measure up to these specifications. "For, if society is continued on a democracy based on universal suffrage, its existence depends upon the volume and intensity of interest its political processes can arouse."

A recent study made on education in the United States has this to say regarding the problems of adult education:

"The number who cannot come to a reasoned conclusion on the problems with which they must deal as voting citizens and economic producers and consumers is very large. To understand his economic environment the citizen must have at least an elementary knowledge of such important problems as production, consumption, and distribution of commodities; transportation and communication; capital and labor; money and credit; charities and correction. As a voting citizen he must pass upon a wide range of vital questions affecting national, State, and local government. As the head of a family, he needs an appreciation of health, child welfare, money management, and community responsibility. To these broader concepts adult education of the future will address itself."

If we believe H. G. Wells when he said that the future history of the world may well be a race between education and disaster, we may well ask what hope can there be for a country, the majority of whose citizens do not proceed beyond the seventh or eighth grade. But even if they go far beyond that and then lose the habit of learning, the result may be equally disastrous.

Stanley Baldwin in his last visit to this continent said: "Freedom is the air we breathe, freedom is in our blood and bones: the independence of the human spirit. But we are so used to it that if ever we think of it at all, we think it has dropped into our laps like manna from the skies, and unless we go a little beneath the surface in our questioning, we may feel that we enjoy this freedom because we are better than other people and therefore more worthy of it.

"The truth is that the vast majority of our peoples have forgotten that this freedom was bought with a great price: that it was obtained through the struggles of generations of those who went before us, by mental wrestlings, by endurance of persecution, by successive failures and triumphs: and we have entered into their labors, the labors of men far better

than ourselves. And if we realize this, how can we imagine that what has been won at such a price can be maintained without effort and at no cost to ourselves? Can the lamp by the light of which our ancestors trod their upward path still show us the way unless we keep it trimmed and bright when it is handed to us? . . .

"In the totalitarian state the citizen has only to do as he is told; he has not to think, to make a choice: no direct responsibility rests on him . . . Our ideals are harder of accomplishment because they are far higher: they involve the cooperation of men of their own free will endeavoring to work . . . in the raising of mankind . . . As the lights are quenched in one country after another, there is hope in the world so long as our lamps are trimmed and their rays may be seen penetrating the gloom. What a responsibility rests on us!"

And what an added significance have these words taken on as a result of recent events! The race between education and disaster has begun! Perhaps in the contest we can learn something even from our enemies. It is certain that the tremendous driving power of the Germans is due in no small measure to the years of incessant and intensive bombardment of a single set of ideas to which they have been subjected. Can we not learn from that the national importance of more intensive education — an education for constructive rather than destructive purposes? In other words, if Hitler can use ideas to destroy civilization, cannot the democracies, *if they make the effort*, use ideas to rebuild civilization? Can anyone doubt that if we could only employ the same devotion, persistence and intelligence in our democratic planning, we could effect a degree of efficiency far higher than anything achieved by the action of dictators?

Education, therefore, must no longer be something that is laid away with the school books; it must not remain something remote and unrelated to life; it must be a part of life itself if we are to hold our own in a seething world. While not overlooking the essential role of our schools, we must, while seeking to improve the work of the schools, carry our programme beyond the schools and universities into the busy lives of men and women in the world without.

We cannot now save the wasted years. The democracies — civilization itself — must meet a challenge of unparalleled violence and bitterness that imperils not only our material resources, but the very foundations of our faith. Today the British Commonwealth of Nations faces this challenge alone. We are compelled to improvise our defences even under the full force of the attack. Many cannot bear arms in the struggle, but we can all play our part in the battle of ideas by helping to establish a unity

Continued on page 22

AGRICULTURE AND THE WAR
by J. E. Lattimer

The war is causing Canada's export market for farm products to disappear. The expected demand from Britain has not materialized. How can we reorganize our system to meet these changed conditions?

PROSPECTS for a bountiful harvest were seldom better than this season; surpluses of farm products over domestic needs are already available or in prospect. What shall be done with these surpluses depends upon the fortunes of war, which no one at this time dares to predict. Due to the loss of normal export markets the outlook for farming alters from month to month, from week to week, even from hour to hour. Prospects that appear definite and dependable when written down may be completely shattered by the time they appear in print. This makes any discussion of the situation difficult and hazardous. Yet the difficulty is no excuse for trying to avoid mistakes by doing nothing.

CANADIAN SURPLUS

Canadian farming is organized on the foundation of overseas export of its surplus products and Canada, with eleven million people and sixty million acres in field crops, in addition to its pasture lands, is dependent on export outlets. The normal outlet is densely populated Europe. Germany and Italy have about one acre of cropped land per inhabitant while Canada has at least five. Yet Italy is bent on self-sufficiency and has been largely self-sufficient since 1925, when Mussolini started what he called "The Battle of Wheat." Germany also sought the same goal. Both these countries resorted to extreme rationing and regimentation even during the period of preparation for war. They preferred airplanes, tanks and guns to butter!

EUROPE ON A RATION

The swallowing up of other countries by Germany in the past few months has removed from Finland, Norway, Sweden, Holland, Belgium, France and Switzerland the chance of trading overseas. These were the countries that practised, in so far as their environment allowed, the greatest degree of freedom of trade. They are now added to the area compelled to resort to rationing. France, which might have absorbed vast quantities to feed her armies, is also out of the picture. Britain is now almost the only market left, and since the outbreak of war Britain has rationed many leading foods.

USE OF SUBSTITUTES

Many of the countries mentioned were markets for grain and feeds from overseas before they were engulfed, and were at the same time sources of supply of butter, bacon and eggs for Britain. It may seem surprising that the shutting off of these sources of Britain's supply of these pro-

ducts has not increased the demands on Canada more than it has, but there are two reasons for this condition. One is the need for saving shipping space for more essential goods. The other and more important reason is the need for saving money for other things now more urgently needed. The people of Britain must now choose guns in preference to butter or bacon. The loss of Danish and Dutch supplies of butter is being met *not* by increasing imports from Canada, but by resorting to the use of margarine, which may be home manufactured, and the price of margarine is set from sixpence per pound for the lower grade used in cooking, to eightpence per pound for the better grade that is substituted for butter. The better grade at eightpence per pound is available for about fifteen cents per pound in Canadian money. The loss of Danish and Dutch supplies of bacon is *not* met by increasing quota requirements from Canada, but by reducing the allowance, as occurred on June tenth of this year.

DIFFICULTIES OF EXCHANGE

Since the formation of the Dominion it has been the custom for Canada to send surplus farm products to Britain and to take goods from the United States, leaving that country and Britain to square accounts as they might. This worked well while both Canada and the United States were debtor countries, as was the case before the first World War, but recently it has been more difficult. Goods must be paid for in goods, gold, or credit. Since the outbreak of war in September Canada has paid back in goods one hundred million dollars on loans previously made in Britain. This is what bankers term repatriation of loans. The need and opportunity for further financing of sales of goods in this way still exist.

Payments for goods with goods still remains a difficulty. For the twelve months ending April, 1940, the value of goods which Canada sent to Britain was 258 million dollars more than the value of the goods taken in exchange. At the same time Canada imported 185 million dollars more from the United States than was exported to that country, leaving out the item gold. Gold and the income from tourists are now the two chief methods of squaring the balance with the United States. How permanent dependence on these items may prove to be would be even more hazardous to prophesy than the outlook for farming.

Events are rapidly stressing the need of either taking goods for goods or making loans, if overseas trade is to proceed. Surplus food products must either be exchanged for other goods from the countries that take them, or else

Continued on page 23

SCHOOL PROBLEMS AND VIEWPOINTS

GRADUATION DAY IN THE
SCHOOL FOR TEACHERS
by Violet B. A. Ramsey

WE could travel from eastern coast to western shore of this vast Dominion and nowhere could we find a more lovely picture than was seen on the Campus of Macdonald College that day of graduation, with clear blue skies, brilliant sunshine, and a breeze that made the atmosphere of the crowded Assembly Hall bearable. The campus with its green lawns sloping down to the Ottawa River, the masses of foliage and blossom, the fragrance of lilacs and the more subtle perfume of the flower borders and bushes, all formed a perfect setting for the red-roofed buildings which are so well known to the people of our province. Last, but by no means least, came the graduates themselves, men and maidens from all parts of Quebec, yes, some from homes so far away that they had not seen them since they entered college in September.

When we look at this picture and then think of war-torn Europe, the contrast is almost too painful to contemplate. But even into this peaceful scene the shadows of war are creeping, for some of the men graduates who received their diplomas that day are waiting the call to serve King and Country, and that call may have come to them by now.

But the majority of these students are looking forward to the building up of civilization while their classmates strive to stem the destruction of it. Into our large schools in city and town, and into the smaller ones in our rural districts, will come the "new teacher" when school opens in September. These new teachers who graduated that lovely June afternoon have many hopes but also many fears as they face their new responsibilities. And so it is to the fathers and mothers of the province that this appeal is made. Give them a real welcome to your community, show them the sympathy they so much need. They are lonely oftimes, they have left college where they could get advice, help and companions when in difficulties, they have left homes where affection and sympathy surrounded them, and now it is to you they look for all of these.

There are many practical ways in which you can help. Remember your children are spending a large part of their waking hours in that classroom. Help to make it as attractive as possible. A few willing fathers in a community can make that dingy classroom a fitting place for their young folks to enter when school opens. It is not a financial problem at all, it is a partnership of parent and teacher that is needed.

Continued on page 23

THE QUEBEC HOME
AND
SCHOOL COUNCIL

IN several provinces Home and School Associations have been set up with the purpose of providing some organization where parents and teachers can meet on common ground and get a better understanding of each other's problems and points of view. Such organizations can greatly hasten the movement for better schools, and the creation of more of these Associations in Quebec is very desirable.

Some central organization is also necessary; one that will link together the different Associations, and that can deal with problems of a provincial rather than a purely local nature; that can direct activities of common interest and prepare material for the study of school improvement and organization. But this central organization should include other groups than the individual Home and School Associations — groups like the Women's Institutes, the Provincial Association of Protestant School Boards, the Provincial Association of Protestant Teachers, the High School Principals' Association, to name but a few who are all interested in the same thing. All these would have valuable contributions to make to the work of a Central Council.

And this Council is now in existence. The framework was laid in Montreal by a joint committee of the Protestant Committee of Public Instruction and the Mental Hygiene Institute, and their recommendations were presented at a largely attended meeting of interested persons held at Macdonald College on June 27th, where the following resolution was adopted: "that a Quebec Provincial Council be formed at this meeting and that organization plans for such a Council be immediately carried out."

Provisional officers elected at the meeting were: President, Dr. W. H. Brittain; 1st Vice-President, Mr. Leslie Buzzell; 2nd Vice-President, Mrs. R. Thomson; Secretary, Mr. Herbert Gilbert; Treasurer, Miss Alice Dresser. An executive committee was also named, consisting of Mrs. H. Moore, Mr. D. E. Pope, Mrs. Donald Bailey, Mr. Alex. Sim, Dr. Harry Hall, Mrs. A. Stalker, Mrs. Cameron Dow, Mrs. Kuhring, Mrs. W. T. B. Mitchell, and the President of the P.A.P.T. (Miss Truax). The officers and members of the executive committee were charged with the responsibility of drawing up a constitution for the new Council, to be presented for ratification at a future meeting.

COOPERATION AND MARKETING
A page of interest to the members of farmers' cooperatives.
RURAL COOPERATIVES OF QUEBEC
by H. C. Bois

COOPERATION is not a recent invention. It is neither a philanthropic nor a charitable institution. It is a practical system with high humanitarian ideals; a doctrine of peace and social justice.

Cooperation has looked ahead. It is as far removed from Communism as it is from Capitalism. The cooperative movement does not resort to violence. No one has ever seen the cooperators of any country marching armed through the streets. The timid can reassure themselves, for it is not the members of the cooperative societies who disturb their rest. It is ridiculous and at the same time absolutely false to pretend that the Cooperative movement leans towards Socialism or Communism. Such a statement shows either a wild imagination or else bad faith. On the contrary, the Cooperative associations, far from retricting human personality, permit it to develop to the fullest extent. To quote Dr. Fauquet, ex-chief of the Cooperative Service of the International Labour Bureau, "It permits a common action which has at one and the same time the requirement and the aim of individual autonomy and independence." Anyone who wishes to do so may join a cooperative society, and in this organization money is reduced to its proper role, that of a servant to whom a salary is paid, not that of a master to whom all is handed over. The control of this society is divided equally amongst its members and profits are distributed to each member in proportion to the amount of business he has transacted through the Society. It is because it is directed towards the individual that cooperation knows no frontiers. We find it everywhere in the world, and in every country the Cooperative organizations are inspired by the same principles. It is only in their methods of action that we find any difference; of necessity they must adapt themselves to differing conditions created by politics, economic systems and the laws of each nation.

THE BEGINNINGS OF COOPERATION

Before giving a brief description of the Cooperative movement in rural Quebec it might be well to summarize the development of Cooperatives in the world. We are accustomed to say that cooperation dates back to 1844 with the founding of the Rochdale Society in England. The historian can easily discover, farther back in the past, organizations which correspond very closely to cooperatives as we know them today. However, let us start with 1844. Twenty-eight workers living in a poverty which occurs only in the worst cases today, opened a store on December 21st. Its inventory was as follows:—

22 lbs. butter
50 lbs. sugar
6 bags flour
1 bag oatmeal
2 dozen candles

No store and no beginning could have been more modest, and yet this Society was the beginning of an organization which has today attained a remarkable development. There are now more than 1000 English Co-operatives with a membership of over 8,000,000, and annual business of over a billion and a quarter dollars. Such results demonstrate the value of the basic principles and administrative methods adopted by Cooperatives. This progress was made in the face of strong opposition on the part of manufacturers and merchants, who more than once brought political power to their assistance.

COOPERATION AT HOME AND ABROAD

To give some exact idea of the strength of the movement in the world we may cite some statistics taken from "Cooperative Information" published by the International Labour Bureau at Geneva, Sept. 26th, 1939. Throughout the world, with the exception of Soviet Russia, there were 426,760 agricultural cooperatives with an active member-ship of approximately 45,500,000, and 24,685 consumers cooperatives with some 20,00,000 members. The statisticians have included with the agricultural cooperatives, Credit Unions, as long as the latter are concerned with rural economic life. A number of these Credit Unions also carry on commercial activities, but the majority of pur. chases of agricultural supplies and the sales of agricultural products are carried on by cooperatives specializing in this line of activity. From the same source of information we discover that 172,182 agricultural cooperatives purchase goods for their members and that the total value of the goods is approximately $644,849,882.00. The sales of 174,513 selling cooperatives came to $2,826,625,900.00.

And what have we at home? Once more a little history. We said in the beginning that cooperation was not a new thing. In fact, the first Mutual Fire Insurance Company was organized at Huntingdon about 1854. Between this date and 1900 organizations of butter factory and cheese factory patrons were fairly numerous. Several of these associations drew up regulations which might very well be used today without any changes. One of the first Co-operative Societies, organized even before the province has any special legislation, was that at Adamsville, founded in 1903 by Abbe J. A. B. Allaire. However, up until 1910 not many new organizations were formed.

Continued on page 23

THE COLLEGE PAGE

Items of news regarding the College, staff members, students and graduates.

THE DEGREE COURSE

REGISTRATION day for degree students will be on September 27th. In spite of the war, of enlistments for war service and of changes in plans due to the general situation, the prospects indicate a fair enrollment. It is generally agreed that students too young for military duty, or not available for war service, will do well to continue their studies, since future opportunities for untrained men are likely to be slight.

Macdonald College offers a university training of high quality at a much lower cost than at many of the larger institutions. Scientific courses leading to later specialization in some phase of technical agriculture, or in one of the basic sciences, offer a broad training that does not necessarily tie a student down to any narrow field, but gives him an opportunity to enter various professions or industries if his tastes run in that direction. Household Science is becoming an increasingly popular profession for women students, offering as it does training in a field where male competition is at a minimum.

Both men and women students, while carrying on their studies, may assist in the war effort and prepare themselves for possible future service. Red Cross groups are in operation which any of the women students may join, and the Macdonald Company of the McGill Contingent of the C.O.T.C. welcomes any recruits from among the men students.

THE DIPLOMA COURSE

SINCE its foundation Macdonald College has been interested in and has actively supported better farming methods and a better farm community. To assist in better farming methods a great amount of research work has been successfully carried on in many lines. New varieties of seed have been developed, new knowledge on the feeding and management of livestock has been brought to light, our knowledge of soils and fertilizers has been broadened and in numerous other ways contributions have been made which have tended to make things easier for the farmer.

To assist in the development of a better farm community an equally great effort has been made. Courses are provided to meet the needs and provide opportunity for the farm boy — The Degree course for those who wish to follow a professional scientific training and the Diploma course for those boys who desire to farm but who have not had the opportunity to carry on with their education. This latter course has been popular and well supported by our farm boys. There is not an English speaking district in Quebec which has not sent someone in the past; in recent years,

while we expected more, the response has been quite satisfactory. This has had a very pronounced effect in most communities. In this connection, I am reminded of a field day I attended recently. The programme had been organised by the county agronome, but the main events were being handled by former Diploma students! Two boys gave a demonstration of judging dairy type cattle, while others took part in the sports and recreational features. The work was well done and the whole affair very successful. All Diploma boys do not receive as much from their course of training as those particular boys, but they do get something very worthwhile. One cannot attend many functions in any district of Quebec without meeting former students of the Diploma Course. These boys are helping to develop a healthy agriculture and a more satisfactory community life. Their influence has become widespread.

Being able to read and write is not sufficient. Farming is so many-sided, it demands a much broader training than can be given in the local school. We must broaden the outlook, become more familiar with the many problems of fertility and production and establish an interest in these problems before we can develop real farmers.

To the farm boys in Quebec an opportunity is available when employment on the farm is at a low ebb. The cost is reasonable. May we hope that a larger and larger number will continue to take advantage of it.

PROFESSOR HODGINS ON LEAVE

WHEN the Agricultural Supplies Board was organized shortly after the outbreak of war, the University was asked by the Federal Government to release Prof. S. R. N. Hodgins from his duties at Macdonald College so that he could act as Secretary of the new organization.

The Board acts with Dominion and Provincial agencies and allied Boards as the directing agency in coordinating Canada's war-time agricultural programme, with its chief aim to see that the food and fibre supplies needed by Canada and her allies are available. Any reorganization of farming made necessary by war needs is being planned so as to leave the Canadian farmer, as far as possible, in a position to follow his normal programme when peace returns.

Professor Hodgins graduated from Macdonald College with a B.S.A. degree in 1920, and has been on the staff of the College for many years as Assistant Professor of English. He was perhaps best known outside the College in his capacity as a writer, and as the editor of the Journal of Agriculture, a position he held until the withdrawal of the Journal in 1936. With this background Mr. Hodgins brings to his new and responsible position a wealth of experience of agricultural affairs.

PROFESSOR SUMMERBY HONOURED

PROFESSOR ROBERT .SUMMERBY, M.S.A., Head
of the Department of Agronomy at Macdonald College,
was elected a life member of the Canadian Seed Growers'
Association at the meeting held at Winnipeg, June 17th to
19th. This honour was conferred "for his contribution to
the Canadian Seed Growers' Association and to Canadian
agriculture."

Mr. Summerby was born at Lachute, Argenteuil
County, Que., and received his early education at Lachute
Academy. He obtained the degree of B.S.A. at Macdonald
College, being a member of the first graduating class, and
later took postgraduate work at Cornell University where
he obtained the degree of M.S.A. On his graduation from
Macdonald College in 1911 he was appointed to the staff
of the Agronomy Department where he was in charge of
cereal breeding until 1919, when he became head of the
department. During his association with the College he has
been responsible for originating several important new
varieties.

As Chairman of the Quebec Seed Board, a position
which he has held since 1923, Mr. Summerby has taken a
leading part in the advancement of field crop work in
Quebec, a service which has been increased by his membership in many other committees having to do with the
advancement of agriculture in that field.

He has been associated with the Canadian Seed Growers'
Association for 20 years and has had much to do with
shaping the policies of that organization and in developing
regulations concerning the multiplication and distribution
of pedigreed varieties in a pure form. He has been active
on many of the committees of the Association, including
those on by-laws, regulations, standards, causes of con-
tamination, registration, etc. Prof. Summerby was Vice-
President of the C.S.G.A. from 1920 until 1933, President
from 1933 to 1936, Honourary Vice-President until the
present, and has represented the Province of Quebec on the
directorate for many years.

NOTES ABOUT GRADUATES

THE second generation is now graduating from Macdonald College. Grant Parent, a 1940 graduate, is the
son of L. V. Parent '12' who is manager of the Lennoxville
Branch of the Co-operative Wool Growers' Association.

Margaret Hetherington, daughter of T. A. Hetherington,
B.S.A., '17 was granted her degree in Household Science
in 1940.

In 1939 Wilma Scott, daughter of Mrs. S. J. Scott
(Marion Waters, a former School for Teachers student)
received the bachelor's degree in Household Science.

Dr. Robert Newton, a native of Quebec, who was
graduated from Macdonald College in 1912, has been
appointed Dean of the Faculty of Agriculture of the
University of Alberta. For a short time following gradua-
tion he was Macdonald College Demonstrator at Shawville
in Pontiac County. Since 1932 he has been in charge of the
Division of Biology and Agriculture of the National
Research Council. He now returns to the University of
Alberta where he formerly was professor in charge of the
Department of Biochemistry and Agronomy.

Morley Honey, one of the Macdonald College Advisory
Committee, is a former student. He is farming at Abbots-
ford, specializing in orcharding. The apple production is
combined with dairy and beef herds, so that a better use of
labour and of land can be made. A son of Mr. Honey's
has successfully followed the work of the Diploma Course
in Agriculture.

Near Howick and within a radius of a few miles four
brothers, former students of Macdonald College, are successfully conducting farms. Earl and Bruce Ness both
followed the four year course in Agriculture. The two other
brothers, Douglas and Mitchell, completed the Diploma
Course. The Ness family are satisfied that special training
in agriculture added to practical experience is worthwhile.

The Honourable J. Sydney Dash, B.S.A. 1913, now
Director of Agriculture for British Guiana, and Mr. H. W.
Clay, B.S.A. 1922, of the Department of Agriculture in
Prince Edward Island, were recent visitors to the College.

Honour Roll

We publish herewith the names of those Macdonald
College students and graduates whom we know to be
serving with His Majesty's forces. If any of our readers
know of any others whose names should be included, the
Editor would welcome information.

Archer, P. L.	Hughes, G. S.
Burnell-Jones, E. C. B.	Knighton, G. S.
Cannon, D. G.	Leonard, E. M.
Carlos-Clarke, A.	McKinnel, R.
Colley, J.	Musset, D. S.
Creelman, D. W.	O'Callaghan, B.
Dunn, J. A.	Pope, F. N.
Gilman, G. B.	Reeves, A. J.
Gleadall, G.	Seed, J. R. W.
Griffen, P.	Shewell, G. E.
Gordon, R.	Smith, K. H.
Hanna, W. J.	Varney, M. E.
Harrison, W. L. E.	Walker, A. H.
Harvey, D.	Watson, Jas.
	Way, C.

SWINE FEEDING

Continued from page 9

VITAMINS

The fourth group of feeds are the vitamin carriers. In the minds of many feeders, vitamins are mysterious substances whose presence or absence may be responsible for almost unbelievable differences in the behavior of the animals fed. To-day, much of the mystery surrounding vitamins has been cleared up by the careful study of experimental animals. This role of most of the recognized vitamins is known. With this greater understanding of the vitamin question, however, has come a fuller appreciation of how essential it is that pig rations shall provide sufficient quantities of these nutrients. The fact that the quantities required are oftentimes very small in no way alters the fact of their importance in regulating the processes which go on in the animal's body. Thus, deficiency of a vitamin may be reflected in the failure of health and growth in the animal thus deprived of these operating essentials.

Within each of the above four groups of feeds there are naturally many feed stuffs and materials. In some cases materials belonging within one group are quite satisfactory substitutes for each other. In other instances each food has its own nutritional characteristics which make it necessary that it be considered individually.

In the next article the common feeds and their special values in the swine ration will be discussed in some detail.

HOW TO CURE . . .

Continued from page 11

It should be remembered that the amount of pull required to pull the twine through the tension at the can should be about 9 pounds, though anywhere from 6 to 12 pounds will usually work well. When testing this pull the twine should be pulled from the eye of the needle.

To pull the twine from the twine disc should require not less than 35 pounds and not more than 40 pounds. In case of trouble test these points, using a small spring balance to measure the pull.

If the Band No. 2 is found with the bundle instead of on the bills the tension of the twine disc spring only is at fault.

Band No. 3. This is found with the bundle, both ends being crimped in an effort on the part of the bills to tie a knot. Either the bill hook spring is too loose, allowing the cords to slip through the bills' grip, or the little hump on the bottom of the upper bill is worn off. If tightening the bills' spring does not help, then examine the hump, and if it seems worn, file the middle away behind it so as to make a hump. Care must be taken not to leave a rough surface; it is better to smooth the steel with emery cloth after filing. If this does not effect a cure get a new bill hook complete with shaft.

Band No. 4. This shows a band ripped from the disc

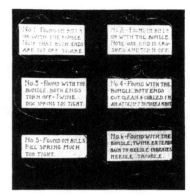

by the bill hook because the disc is so tight that it will not let the twine slip through sufficiently to allow the tying of a knot. It is usually caused by the operator overdoing the adjustment of the tension on the twine disc. Remember, a quarter of a turn at a time is enough.

Band No. 5. Every operator has seen his machine tie a slip noose around the bundle from which the twine was not cut but extended back to the needle; if not noticed at once a long piece of twine may be drawn from the twine box. If it occurs only once in a few days of cutting it is likely due to some strong stemmed weeds having gotten between the end of the needle and the twine disc, preventing the disc from depositing the twine in the notch of the disc. If it occurs more frequently it may mean that weeds are still the cause of it but the reason they interfere is because the needle point is not sharp enough to pierce this weed stuff; a rusty needle point may also have the same effect. If so, the point should be sharpened and brightened. If the trouble is chronic it may be due to a bent needle, the needle may not come up far enough to deposit the twine in the disc, due to a worn needle eye or to wrong adjustment of the needle pitman, or the disc may be out of time. The needle should advance until it touches the breast plate of the knotter, or, in some machines, until it touches the stripper arm. If a test shows that it could advance a little farther the needle pitman should be shortened.

Band No. 6. This is rather an unusual trouble which occurs when the bill hook spring is much too tight and, at the same time, the binder is tying very loose bundles. This combination of conditions allows the stripper arm to pull the cords up through the breast plate instead of pulling them off the bills; the discharge arms kick out the bundles all the same, breaking the twine and leaving the band on the bills. Loosen the tension on the bill hook spring a little at a time.

This also brings up the question as to how to make the binder tie tighter or looser bundles and how to make the bundles smaller or larger. It is impossible to give instructions for the various makes of machine within the scope of a short article, but the following rules hold good for all of them and may correct some wrong impressions that seem to be more or less prevalent. The only way to make the binder tie a tighter bundle is to tighten the trip spring; this is a long coil spring with an adjustment nut on the end of the bolt running through the spring. In the Massey-Harris machine it is located under the middle of the deck while in the Deering, Frost & Wood, John Deere and others, it is located out at the front end of the binding part. Tightening the tension of the twine at the can will never tie a tighter bundle, but will only cause trouble.

The size of the bundles is regulated by the trip lever against which the grain is pushed by the packers. Moving this lever so that the sizes of the space in front of the packer is increased must result in a larger bundle. Moving this lever in towards the needle so as to decrease the space between the packer and the trip lever, means that less grain can be packed in this space and a smaller bundle is the result. In some machines two levers are used in combination to regulate the bundle sizes, but the above principle still holds good.

Every binder should be in good shape before it enters the season's cutting. The time to look it over is before the grain is ripe. Cutting the grain is a job which must be done on time — which means it must be done speedily. To tackle it with a machine not in good condition is disheartening and frequently results in loss of money.

EDUCATION FOR DEMOCRACY
Continued from page 15

of will and purpose among our people, in learning how better to work the processes of democracy. There is still, we hope, room for differences of opinion — but has not the time come for all men who cherish its ideals to bury their differences and unite to defend what is left of our civilization?

To do this we must be prepared to use various instruments and to use them on a national scale. The corner stone of our adult education programme is the small study or discussion club of which many hundreds now exist in Canada. No totalitarian state can tolerate free discussion, for its basic assumption is that its ultimate principles are beyond criticism. *To them criticism and treason are synonymous.* But for any democratic society to survive, an absolute necessity is free discussion, and we must, if we can make ourselves, learn to take part in free discussion, and we must learn to teach to others the art — for it is indeed an art — of constructive discussion of those problems which are vital to the life of the community and of constructive action based on full knowledge of the facts. This movement represents a very different approach from going

among people with the avowed intention of uplifting them. Here they work, study and plan to improve and uplift themselves. Such activities, therefore, should be pursued with added vigour. All organizations supporting our democratic way of life should consolidate their efforts for the common good. All individuals with superior knowledge and training should be prepared to offer the necessary leadership and direction to effect this end.

Many people smugly shelter themselves behind the saying, "the right shall prevail". *But it is a dangerous illusion to imagine that the right can prevail without the devoted efforts of men and women dedicated to the cause of right.* We hear much these days of "fifth columns". It has come as a staggering shock to us to find that there exists in all countries people with totalitarian minds — ruthless, unscrupulous, treacherous minds, who work and plot unceasingly against the things in which we believe. But more insidious than such "fifth columns" are their many unconscious allies, some of whom regard themselves as model citizens. For the foes of democracy are quite as much inertia, selfishness and indifference to social and economic injustice and to political corruption as is outright treachery, with which we now know how to deal. To fight these things is a genuine part of our war effort. Our enemies were willing to accept guns for butter, to endure, not only without grumbling, but even with enthusiasm, deprivations of all sorts, and to follow with fervour and resolution a hard and rigorous régime in order that their ideas should prevail. They shall prevail unless our will and resolution are greater than theirs, unless we too accept sacrifice and hardship in order that our ideals shall triumph. Moral forces are only invincible when supported by the invincible will of men and women devoted to their service!

If we fail to maintain the efficiency of our basic institutions by democratic methods we may yet be forced to submit to a more ruthless and efficient system imposed on us by others. Hard and bitter days lie ahead, but surely now is the time for us to take stock of ourselves, to consolidate our position, to intensify our efforts, to work and to plan that the world for which our sons are willing to give their lives should be one worth saving. If we can play our part in this hour, it may be that we can yet salvage enduring values even from the wreck of empires and play a significant part in rebuilding a broken world.

Eric McGreer, originally from Montreal and who graduated from Macdonald in 1922, has been associate editor of the Farm and Ranch Review for some years. This position he has now left to become Secretary-Treasurer of the Calgary Board of Trade. Mrs. McGreer (Vera Kirby) also is a former Macdonald student.

The editor of the Family Herald and Weekly Star is now R. S. Kennedy, '12. Mr. Kennedy was with the Advertising Promotion Department of the same publication for some years.

AGRICULTURE AND THE WAR

Continued from page 16

supplied on credit. Who furnishes the credit is another question. It is clear that it cannot be the farmer, for he is in no position to furnish credit even for the storing of non-perishable products such as wheat. The pay-as-you-go method of financing war does not promote expansion of supplies, but entails rationing.

THE PRESSURE OF EVENTS

Canadian agriculture is peculiarly dependent on the outcome of the present conflict. If the totalitarian principles prevail, Canada will have to reorganize its agriculture, which is now based on a free market. It has been argued that the totalitarian system cannot be permanent because of the tendency for regimentation to prevent abundance, the devastation and disorganization now proceeding, and the difficulty of farming and fighting at the same time. These last two conditions are modified somewhat by the extent or rapidity with which some countries have been overrun. Hence the expected scarcity of food products on the continent of Europe may not develop to the extent anticipated. The Germans may be expected to exercise their organizing ability to maintain agricultural production to a greater extent than during the last war, both at home and in the countries which they have overrun and, if they can, to form a closed system within that area. It should be pointed out that they now control the output of countries like Denmark and Holland, normally sources of food supply for the British market. If the devastated countries suffer want, either the Germans must look after them or they will have to do without.

We may here point out the great contrast in the method and technique of farming in this country and in Europe. For each worker in farming in Canada in 1931 there were about 77 acres of improved land. For each labourer in farming and forestry in Europe the amount of tillable land available was 4.2 acres in Bulgaria, 5.2 acres in Italy, 6 acres in Poland, 7 acres in Germany and Belgium, 9 acres in Czechoslovakia and Holland, 10 acres in France, 15 acres in Denmark and 32 acres in Britain. The economy of man power in the provision of food makes possible the release of man power for other tasks. This should be one of our greatest advantages over our antagonists in ensuring that freedom may prevail in all things, including trade.

GRADUATION DAY . . .

Continued from page 17

And to the teachers who are looking forward with eagerness to their new work, who are full of hopes and aspirations, we would say—do not allow those dreams of yours to be destroyed; remember you have the making and marring of character as well as the training of the minds of the younger generation in your control. In subsequent

talks to parents and teachers, we will discuss more intimately various phases of the work in home and school and the practical ways in which all may co-operate.

Meanwhile, during those summer months when our land seems to overflow with the abundance of Nature's gifts, let us all take ourselves to task, and in the face of the tremendous events of these days, ask ourselves what we can do with good team work to give our children the best possible chance to prepare themselves for that time which must surely come when our young people will take up the task of building a better world where "none will be afraid but each will think of the other".

Just think of the results which would follow if we could find in every community the spirit suggested by these words written by a principal in a letter to parents. "The greatest gift you can send to school is a cheerful, healthy child, anxious to learn, for us to guide from day to day. We will return him to you each night a little bigger and better, we hope, because of his contact with us."

May this be the mutual aim of all our parents and teachers in the Province of Quebec!

RURAL COOPERATIVES

Continued from page 18

EARLY COOPERATIVE SOCIETIES

The Quebec Syndicates Law was adopted in 1906 and the Cooperative Societies' Law in 1908, but it was not until during the next decade, that is to say from 1910 to 1920, that the movement really began to expand. In 1910, following the annual meeting of the Societé d'Industrie Laitière, the Quebec Cheesemakers Cooperative was established, which was later known as the Coopérative Centrale des Agriculteurs de Québec. In 1913, the Comptoir Coopératif de Montréal appeared. In 1914 the Société Coopérative des Producteurs de Semences de Québec was organized, and in 1916, at a meeting of all the Cooperative societies held at Oka, it was decided to establish a central organization which would be called The Confederation of Co-operative Societies.

The cooperatives of that period noticed that the multiplication of central organizations was dividing their forces, and they began to work to achieve unity. According to information supplied by Mr. Paul Boucher, there were in September, 1920, 50 local cooperatives affiliated with the Confédération des Sociétés Coopératives, 83 affiliated with the Coopérative Centrale des Agriculteurs de Québec; 38 affiliated with the Société Coopérative des Producteurs de Semence, and 76 affiliated with the Comptoir Coopératif de Montreal.

THE COOPERATIVE FEDEREE ORGANIZED

The Confederation disappeared in 1921. The Comptoir Coopératif de Montreal was in difficulties. It seemed to be the proper time to consolidate all these Societies into one.

Therefore, in 1922 at the instigation of the Hon. J. E. Caron, then Minister of Agriculture, the Coopérative Centrale des Agriculteurs de Québec, the Coopérative des Producteurs de Semences de Québec, and the Comptoir Coopératif de Montreal were amalgamated under the name of the Coopérative Fédérée de Québec. This political intervention, which is justifiable from several points of view, was nevertheless the cause of dissension and disputes.

From 1922 until 1929 the fortunes of the Coopérative Fédérée went up and down. In 1929, the Hon. Mr. Perron decided to place the affairs of the Society on a strict business basis, and to entrust its management and responsibility to the farmers. To achieve this result the Minister readjusted the finances and had a law passed reorganizing the central organization. Since then the Coopérative Fédérée has grown from year to year.

In 1930, with the high prices then existing, its business amounted to $7,233,946.32 and 66 societies were affiliated. Since 1938 its business has increased to $11,731,442.51, in spite of a considerable drop in prices, and the Federation has absorbed over 200 societies and syndicates. In 1939 their business amounted to $11,925,000.00.

In 1930 the Farmers' Union organized its own Comptoir Coopératif. This operated until June 1938, when it decided to join the Coopérative Fédérée de Québec. Today there is only one central cooperative society in the province and it now controls 207 societies and syndicates.

PRESENT STATUS OF COOPERATION

This seems a good time to re-emphasize the value of the cooperative movement. We see another proof of this in the number of local societies, whether affiliated with the Cooperative or not, and in the amount of business they transact.

On December 31, 1938, official statistics showed that there were 215 local cooperative societies with a net surplus of $653,382.60. There are also other more or less specialized societies which operate either in the Provincial or in the Federal domain. Among these can be mentioned the Cooperative Canadienne du Bétail, Limitée, the Société des Producteurs de Miel; the Société des Producteurs de Conserves de Montréal; the Société des Producteurs de Lin de Vaudreul-Soulanges; the Société des Producteurs de Lait de Montréal; the Société des Producteurs de Tabac du district de Joliette, the Société des Producteurs de Tabacs Laurentiens, etc.

Our latest information, which is already several months old, shows that there are 296 local societies in the province with 21,296 members and a capital of $1,097,111.00. We are not discussing here the operations of Credit Unions, Mutual Insurance Companies or Consumers Cooperatives. What has been said above relates exclusively to cooperatives which are concerned with buying, selling, preparing and processing of agricultural products. Is it not evident that the farmer is making more and more use of the cooperatives? By their community purchasing of merchandise, cooperatives permit the farmer to reduce his operating costs. They reduce his selling costs and they make possible the preparation and processing of certain products in the best possible manner. The organization of our agriculture is such as to encourage our people to cooperate. In Quebec in general the cultivated areas on every farm is fairly small; official figures show an average of about 75 acres. On the other hand, the system of operation which our people must follow in view of our physical and economic situation is such as to render difficult the practice of monoculture, or even of very much specialization. Our large farm families encourage the raising of a number of different crops on the farm because this offers a means of using the family labour to best advantage, and so most of our farmers operate their farms so as to raise the greatest possible number of products at the same time. It is very seldom that we find any farm where the output of any one thing is large enough that the proprietor can properly equip himself to grade, pack and prepare the crops as should be done. We have too many different things to sell and too little of each. Such variety, although it has its advantage from another point of view, brings the farmer face to face with difficulties when he comes to sell the products, and so he decides to cooperate with others in order to get all his work done.

WHY JOIN A COOPERATIVE SOCIETY?

So far our farmers have entrusted this work to others. Faced with constant reductions in the net revenue of their farms, our farmers have tried to keep these revenues for themselves, and who can blame them? In other words, they want to obtain a greater percentage of the consumer's dollar. They are not trying, as has been falsely said, to raise the prices of agricultural products to unreasonable levels. Not at all. This is what they mean, in the words of a member of a Cooperative Society who was speaking to me the other day — "We are not rich enough to employ as many people as we do. Today we must do ourselves that which we formerly asked others to do for us." I think this shows the real reason why a large number of farmers join Co-operative Societies. After being members of the Society for some time they begin to get fresh ideas and to become imbued with the real cooperative spirit. No one can deny that cooperation is a powerful method of spreading information about better methods of production and processing. The cooperative really unites its followers, and our people realize their strength. Their self-confidence rises and the cooperative principles which inspire them teach them to use this force in a humane, rational and Christian manner.

TO OUR READERS

The first regular number of the Macdonald College Journal will be issued in September. It can continue to appear only if we receive your active support. Fill out the subscription blank and mail it with fifty cents for a year's subscription NOW.

THIS introductory number of the Macdonald College Journal has been issued as a sample to show you the kind of material you will find in the future copies. The sections for the Department of Agriculture, the Women's Institutes, School Problems and Viewpoints, Cooperation and Designs for Learning will appear each month. In addition we will print timely articles on agricultural subjects; the policies and plans of the Dominion and Provincial Governments will be explained so that our readers will keep in touch with what is going on. We hope to make the Journal interesting and valuable to everyone.

Please read this number through carefully. If you have any comment to make, or if you have any suggestions for future issues, the Editor will be glad to hear from you. And to make sure that you receive the first regular issue in September, send in your subscription without delay, either through the agent in your district or by using the subscription blank on this page.

SUBSCRIPTION FORM

Please send the Macdonald College Journal for one year to

Name...

Print name and address clearly

Address...

The subscription fee of 50c is enclosed.

Fill out this form and mail it with your subscription to:

THE MACDONALD COLLEGE JOURNAL
MACDONALD COLLEGE, QUE.